This book is dedicated to my mother.

Sing…dance…Don't worry about who's watching. Let yourself go and get lost in the music.

Be mindful not to judge someone within the first 5 seconds of meeting them. In 5 months, a kind heart could become the most attractive person in your world.

Why wait until retirement to enjoy your life?
Make enough to live comfortably and travel.
Never look back.

Why are we so afraid of rejection? What's the worst that could happen? It's better to have taken the chance than to never have known.

Don't spend your life trying to compete with anyone else. The competition is only with yourself.

Be conscious not to become so engrossed in your career that you forget to focus on your personal life. Life is better shared.

Enjoy your youth. You are not as fat as you think and you are more beautiful than you could ever imagine.

If you want to have children, don't put it off.
Angels do exist.

Be kind to your siblings. They are the longest connection to your past and the people most likely to be there for you in the future.

See the world. Learn to appreciate different cultures. Understand that not everyone is as fortunate as you and those who appear more fortunate, may not be as blessed.

Know that diet and exercise will lead you to a healthy lifestyle, but understand that mindfulness is just as important.

Give to those less fortunate than you. If you were in their shoes, you would be grateful for the help. Learn to be selfless. One day, you may need someone to do the same for you.

Have no regrets, nor be anxious about the future. Enjoy the present moment, for these are the memories you will keep.

Choose your career wisely. Most people work 8 hours a day, 40 hours a week, and 252 days a year. Do what you have a passion for and it won't feel like work.

Social media may make you think that everyone is happier than you. Truth is that everyone has troubles, sometimes far worse than yours. Count your blessings instead.

Try not to be so frugal with your spending.
A gift can go a long way to show your
appreciation for someone.

Find a partner who makes you happy. Know your worth and don't settle for less.

Choose your attitude every day. Though it may be difficult, a bad attitude will affect no one else but you.

Show envy, but don't be jealous. Jealousy will only make a fool out of you. Others will thrive and you will get left behind.

Keep the junk food at bay. Look after your body which will take care of your mind. Walk.

Have no regrets. Understand that nobody's life is perfect and learning from your mistakes will only make you stronger.

Understand that bullies target happy people to deflect from their own misery. Try not to take it personally. When you're gone, there will always be another victim.

Be brave enough not to follow the crowd. If you notice any wrongdoing, speak up. The world would be a better place with less sheep.

Don't be so quick to believe rumours. Judge people as you see them. People tell lies to deflect from their own truths. Let karma take care of them.

Be careful who you trust. Not everyone has your best interests at heart.

We are taught to believe that there are many different kinds of people in this world. Truth is, there are only two kinds of people; the good and the bad. Keep the good ones close.

A wise woman once said, "Always be the bigger person." It will help you through your disagreements. Choose your arguments wisely.

Believe that you have more than one talent. People are born with many talents. Make the time to explore them all.

Take care of your parents if they took care of you. There is no better medicine than love.

Don't let anyone underestimate your intelligence. Believe in your own abilities and work hard to achieve your goals.

Marry someone with a kind heart. Looks don't last very long.

Be proud of all your achievements. Only you know what you've been through and what it took to get you there.

Show compassion towards the elderly. They were young once too and we will all be old one day. Offer your seat on the bus. Little acts of kindness can make someone's day.

Don't boast or live your life to impress other people. They'll remember you for your acts of kindness, not for your bank balance.

When you ask how someone is, mean it. If you see someone struggling, offer them a friendly ear. It could be just enough to let them know that someone cares.

Learn to forgive those who deserve it. Make peace with your past. It isn't healthy to hold onto grudges.

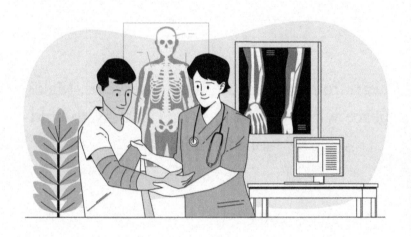

Look after yourself first. You won't be much use to someone else if you don't take care of yourself.

Try not to worry about what other people think of you. They may spare you a thought, but they are far too busy thinking about their own problems.

Learn to be tolerant. No one is perfect, not even you. But set healthy boundaries and don't suffer fools.

Wear sunscreen, come rain or sun. Your ageing skin will thank you for it later.

Practise self-care. Keep your head held high and your confidence will shine through.

Believe in your dreams and work hard to manifest them. A life filled with dreams makes it all the more worthwhile.

Don't believe that your colleague who works overtime and eats lunch at her desk is smarter than you. This only leads to sickness. The smartest people will work efficiently and be the most productive.

You may think that your neighbour who wakes up at 5am every morning and trains 7 days a week is better than you. Scientists will tell you that genetics determine whether you're a morning person or a night owl.

Choose a career you love and it will pay you
in more ways than one.

Show love to your family and friends. A life filled with love is a life well-lived.

Never underestimate the power of love.

Thank you so much for making it this far. I grately appreciate the time you took to read my book. As a small indie publisher, it means alot and I hope I am making a difference in your life's journey.

If you have 60 seconds, reading your honest feedback on Amazon would mean the world to me. It does wonders for the book and I love reading about your experience with it.

To leave your feedback:
1. Open your camera app
2. Point your mobile device at the QR code below
3. The review page will appear in your web browser.

Or visit: rebrand.ly/boz7kqs

Thank you!

Printed in Great Britain
by Amazon